Polyethnicity and N
in World Hi

WILLIAM H. M(

Schools have taught us to expect that people should live in separate national states. But the historical record shows that ethnic homogeneity was a barbarian trait; civilized societies mingled peoples of diverse backgrounds into ethnically plural and hierarchically ordered polities.

The exception was northwestern Europe. There, peculiar circumstances permitted the preservation of a fair simulacrum of national unity while a complex civilization developed. The ideal of national unity was enthusiastically propagated by historians and teachers even in parts of Europe where mingled nationalities prevailed. Overseas, European empires and zones for settlement were always ethnically plural; but in northwestern Europe the tide has turned only since about 1920, and now diverse groups abound in Paris and London as well as in New York and Sydney. Age-old factors promoting the mingling of diverse populations have asserted this power, and continue to do so even when governments in the ex-colonial lands of Africa and Asia are trying hard to create new nations within what are sometimes quite arbitrary boundaries.

In demonstrating how unusual and transitory the concept of national ethnic homogeneity has been in world history, William McNeill offers an understanding that may help human minds to adjust to the social reality around them.

WILLIAM H. McNEILL is Robert A. Millikan Distinguished Service Professor of History, University of Chicago.

# Polyethnicity and National Unity in World History

The Donald G. Creighton
Lectures
1985

## WILLIAM H. McNEILL

UNIVERSITY OF TORONTO PRESS
Toronto Buffalo London

© University of Toronto Press 1986
Toronto Buffalo London
Printed in Canada

ISBN 0-8020-5730-6 (cloth)
ISBN 0-8020-6643-7 (paper)

Canadian Cataloguing in Publication Data

McNeill, W. H. (William Hardy), 1917–
Polyethnicity and national unity in world history
(The Donald G. Creighton lectures ; 1985)
Includes index.
ISBN 0-8020-5730-6 (bound). – ISBN 0-8020-6643-7 (pbk.)
1. Pluralism (Social sciences) – History.
2. Multiculturalism – Canada – History.* 3. Nationalism –
History. 4. Nationalism – Canada – History.
I. Title. II. Series.
JC311.M35 1986        323        C86-094479-4

# Foreword

**D**ONALD CREIGHTON was one of Canada's foremost national historians. I first learned of him through his books, which excited me, like so many Canadians, with the drama of our history. He wrote with a passion and a style that few anywhere could equal. His writings about people, nation, and empire shaped the understanding of a generation of Canadians about their past. Later I was fortunate to become a member of his graduate seminar at the University of Toronto where he instilled the virtues of imagination, research, and controversy in his students. He was a superb teacher, always interested and always demanding, who helped to train many of the professional historians now at work in Canadian universities.

After his death in 1979, a group of family, past students, and friends, inside and outside academe, under the direction of the Honourable Pauline McGibbon, collected monies to establish a special lectureship in his memory. The purpose of the Donald Grant Creighton Lectures is to bring to the University of Toronto a distinguished scholar in the field of history to deliver a series of public lectures on a topic of general interest which, where appropriate, will be published as a book. The hope is that such a contribution to the life of the university and the profession will stand as a legacy to a man who was throughout his life devoted to the pursuit and the expression of knowledge.

Donald Creighton loved grand themes. That was one reason why the selection committee asked Professor William McNeill of the University of Chicago to inaugurate the lecture series. Professor McNeill is a world historian whose work has delved into many aspects of the human experience. Among his many books, for example, are *The Rise of the West* (1963), *Europe's Steppe Frontier, 1500–1800* (1964), *Venice, the Hinge of Europe 1081–1797* (1974), *Plagues and Peoples* (1976), *A World History* (3rd edition, 1979), and *The Pursuit of Power* (1982). At various points in his career, he has been a Fulbright Research Scholar, chairman of his department at the University of Chicago, a Guggenheim Fellow, George Eastman Visiting Professor at Oxford, and a president of the American Historial Association.

Professor McNeill chose as his theme for these lectures the problem of nationality and community, a problem which Donald Creighton had tackled throughout his career as a Canadian historian. Professor McNeill treats this issue in a world context: his account begins with the first empires of recorded history and reaches up to the present day. The result is an imaginative and persuasive description of the way in which different peoples have struggled with ethnic diversity, or in the Canadian context 'multiculturalism,' in their efforts to build stable political units. It is unlikely that Donald Creighton would have agreed with the interpretation that Professor McNeill places upon events. But I am also sure that Donald Creighton would have enjoyed the exercise. He was a man who relished a good argument.

Paul Rutherford
Chairman
Department of History
University of Toronto

# Contents

# LECTURE ONE

## Empire and Nation to 1750

# Empire and Nation to 1750

To INAUGURATE the Creighton lectures at the University of Toronto is a real honor though my qualifications for the role are oddly ironic in ways Donald Grant Creighton might, or might not, approve. I know only his books; and attained that acquaintance after accepting the lectureship, not before. But I wonder what he would think of me and of the committee that chose a lapsed Canadian to lecture in his name. Such a choice might well grate on Creighton's nationalist sensibilities; but there is worse to follow, for what the committee did not know is that I am also descended from William S. McNeill, one-time Speaker of the House in Prince Edward Island, who helped to keep the island out of the Canadian confederation in 1867 because, according to family tradition, he had discovered that Macdonald drank

whiskey and was in this and other respects untrust-
worthy.

But irony was part of Creighton's armory, and the
committee members who invited me, in resorting to
the same weapon, perhaps unknowingly, may nonetheless have been loyal to his memory and faithful to his
personality inasmuch as they invited controversy in
looking beyond Canadian borders for this inaugural
lectureship. They certainly took a risk. It is up to me
now to earn the honor by finding something worthwhile to say.

The title for these lectures is 'Polyethnicity and National
Unity in World History.' My idea was to put con-
temporary Canadian experience of the problems of
French-English coexistence into the broadest possible
historical framework, providing a perspective that will
show polyethnicity as normal in civilized societies,
whereas the ideal of an ethnically unitary state was
exceptional in theory and rarely approached in practice.

Let me begin with reminiscence. As a boy, I attended
Huron Street school, a few blocks from where these
lectures are being delivered, and imbibed a naively
British version of Canadian history. We sang 'Oh
Canada' each morning before classwork began, if I
remember aright, and my conception of the 'true north
strong and free' was nourished by stories about
selected episodes from the War of 1812, featuring
General Brock, Lundy's Lane, and Laura Secord. The
French and Indians were part of Canada's past all right:
Champlain, Radisson and Groseilliers, Montcalm,
together with Hurons torturing Jesuits. But they all
had the grace to meet defeat at the right time, in order

to assume a proper place as subordinate, almost invisible, subjects of the king and members of the British Commonwealth. In this, the French and Indians were conspicuously superior to the Americans, who had the audacity to suppose that they had won not only the War of Independece but the War of 1812 and the Great War as well, whereas Canadians knew that we had won in 1812 and had, with Britain and France, borne the brunt of the conflict in 1914–18.

This school-book portrait of Canadian reality was supplemented by summers in PEI on my grandfather's farm, where real live Frenchmen lived in bleak fishing villages by the shore, a few miles down the road. Contacts between the Scots farmers and the French fishermen were minimal. But I recall my relatives' disdain for what they perceived as French shiftlessness and superstition, as well as their distrust of English upper-class pretentions, associated with the Conservative party and overly refined, la-di-da parlor manners.

So my Canada was not quite the same as Creighton's; and when I departed for the rich, corrupt yet fascinating republic to the south – in 1927, the same year that Donald Creighton returned from Oxford to take up his professorial career at Toronto – I was inoculated against American nationalism as purveyed in Chicago schools, but gradually relinquished or at least modulated the ethnic and other loyalties associated with my initial exposure to a Scottish, Liberal brand of Canadianism. Thus the move from Toronto to Chicago effectually blighted my normal childhood acculturation to local, North American forms of nationalist and ethnic in-group sentiment, and made the ideal of ecumenical detachment easier to attain, or at least to strive for.

Creighton responded to the perennial problem of Canadian identity differently, affirming Canadian and British values against all comers, sometimes with more vigor than charity. That is what makes my presence here so questionable: have I not betrayed Donald Creighton's deepest convictions? But in repudiating his particular answer, simultaneously I intend to affirm the critical importance of addressing the question of who 'we' are, and how lines between 'us' and 'them' are to be drawn.

My fundamental thesis is that the Canadian public experience of polyethnicity on the one hand and of ambivalence towards a richer and more powerful neighbor on the other is shared with most of the rest of the world throughout recorded history. Marginality and pluralism were and are the norm of civilized existence. Metropolitan centers were and are necessarily exceptional, though they do command more than their share of attention in surviving records. And ethnic political unity, even among barbarians, was often illusory and always fragile, because military conquests and other encounters perennially resulted in mixing one sort of people with others.

I propose to disregard ambivalence vis-à-vis some richer and more powerful metropolitan center and concentrate on the other theme, largely because most of us still harbor traces of the idea so deliberately inculcated in Huron Street school half a century ago, to the effect that it is right and proper and normal for a single people to inhabit a particular piece of territory and obey a government of their own devising, whereas it is my contention that civilized societies have nearly always subordinated some human groups to others of a different ethnic background, thereby creating a laminated polyethnic structure. The idea that a government rightfully should rule only over citizens of a single ethnos took root haltingly in western Europe, beginning in the late middle ages; it got into high gear and became fully conscious in the late eighteenth century and flourished vigorously until about 1920; since which time the ideal has unquestionably begun to weaken in western Europe, where it began, but in other parts of the world, especially in the ex-colonial lands of Africa and Asia, it has continued to find fertile ground. I propose to divide my lectures accordingly: beginning today with a sketch of conditions before about 1750; next time offering an analysis of the heyday of European nationalism and its impact on the world at large; and in the final lecture making some remarks about the situation since 1920 and the changing dynamics of political practice in our time.

The strength and weakness of civilizations arose from occupational specialization. The most prominent specialist roles of early times were those of priest and warrior; but professional artisans and traders also played their part in ancient Mesopotamia and Egypt and other early civilizations. Traders who traveled long distances moved among strangers at least part of the time, and some artisan trades, metallurgy in particular, were developed and handed down by itinerant or semi-itinerant bands of smiths, who went wherever ore and fuel could be found and kept the secrets of their skill to themselves while working amongst aliens.

But the politically significant specialization was military. Sumerian and Egyptian civilizations, the earliest on record, both began with conquest: Sumerians came from the south by sea to subjugate the 'Black headed people' of the Mesopotamian marshes; and the first Egyptian Pharaoh, Narmer, also came from the south to subjugate the inhabitants of the Nile delta. The role of religion was certainly important, but the religious ideas and priestly practice of these early civilizations ratified military success by interpreting it as a sign of divine favor. Thus logic and practical advantage both required the gods' servants, the priests, to support the victor, whoever he might be. As a result, even when Semitic-speaking tribesmen conquered the Sumerian cities of Mesopotamia, towards the close of the third millennium BC, the religious establishment accommodated itself to the new rulers; and when sovereignty moved upriver to Babylon, the ancient Sumerian pantheon was adjusted to make Marduk, the local deity of Babylon, supreme among the gods.

The irruption first of Semitic tribesmen from the western desert fringes of Mesopotamia and then, after about 1800 BC, of northern barbarians issuing ultimately from the steppelands of Eurasia marked a fundamental diversification of human ecological and social systems. The nomads, depending initially on sheep and donkeys, and then in the north on cattle and horses, developed a pattern of life that emphasized the military virtues of courage and obedience. Only so could a group safeguard its flocks and herds from predatory animals, and from human raiders as well. In addition, the mobility inherent in nomadism made concentration of fighting manpower comparatively easy to achieve, especially after horseback-riding became the normal way to exploit the speed and strength of horseflesh. This 'cavalry revolution,' beginning, so far as surviving evidence allows us to know, in Assyria about 850 BC, took about five hundred years to spread across the entire Eurasian steppe, establishing itself in the Far East among China's barbarian neighbors by 350 BC, or thereabouts.

During the ensuing two millennia, until the seventeenth century AD, steppe nomads enjoyed persistent military superiority over civilized defenders, being able to move faster, concentrate more rapidly, and live on the countryside more easily than their slower-moving opponents. Rivalries among adjacent tribes, exacerbated by struggles over pasturelands, which in the nature of things could only be occupied and firmly defended for part of the year, often nullified the nomads' inherent military advantage over agricultural populations. Often skillful diplomacy and the policy of 'Hire a thief to catch a thief' allowed civilized peoples to guard their frontiers effectively against nomad incursion. Even when that failed, local defenses, thick on the ground and carefully organized and equipped, could make raiding from the steppe costly and unattractive. But maintenance of such defenses required social and economic arrangements that civilized peoples found difficult to sustain, whereas a successful nomad chieftain could quickly build up a formidable army simply by accepting others into the ranks of his followers. In such circumstances, success bred success. Raids into civilized lands quickly turned into conquest, since the advantages of regulated exactions, i.e., taxes, as against unregulated plunder that was liable to destroy the wealth-producing peasantry were obvious to all concerned in a world in which tax collection was an already established institution.

The consequence of the military prowess of nomads

and their advantages of mobility in war was that most civilized governments in Europe and western Asia, and some in China as well, originated among peoples deriving directly or indirectly from the steppe. This pattern dates back to the Indo-European expansion into Europe and India, long before the cavalry revolution raised nomad military superiority to a new height. A parallel movement of Semitic-speaking invaders and conquerors from Arabia began even earlier, as we have seen, and continued into quite recent times, as one nomad group after another spread northward into the settled lands of the Middle East and westward across Africa, both north and south of the Sahara.

Arab expansion attained a new impetus from the third century AD when a copious supply of domesticated camels began to supplement and extend mobility across hot deserts. Mohammed's revelation, in the seventh Christian century, added a new element, and by uniting Arab tribesmen as never before, provoked one of the most spectacular and rapid conquests of recorded history, and one which, unlike most nomad military successes, also altered cultural and religious alignments in a way that endures to the present.

As far as the Old World is concerned, therefore, the rise of nomadry as a way of life distinct from agriculture acted on the peoples of Eurasia like an enormous gristmill, mixing conquerors with conquered in an ever-changing swirl, and grinding the peasant majority exceeding hard since it was they who suffered plunder and paid taxes, sustaining their military masters and all the other occupational specialists who congregated in cities and maintained the arts and skills of civilization. The peasantries' principal recompense was the dubious privilege of being safeguarded (more or less and some of the time) from even more predatory exactions of some new rival raider and robber.

However unjust this style of civilized society may seem to modern sensibilities, it nonetheless survived and even tended to spread onto new ground. Several factors assured this result, not least among them the superior wealth and power that civilized skills and occupational specialization permitted. The fact that only a few enjoyed wealth and exercised power in such societies did not alter the fact that civilized wealth and power were real and attractive to peoples round about who did what they could to acquire the skills and organization needed to imitate their civilized neighbors and contemporaries. For this reason, civilized forms of society sporadically extended to new ground from the first tiny lodgments in the river valleys of the Near East; and when comparable social structures emerged in the New World and elsewhere, they, too, tended to expand geographically for the same reason.

There was, however, another dimension to civilized society which also contributed to its expansion and is of especial concern to me here because it, too, like the differentiation between nomad and cultivator, assured a continual mix of alien populations in and around the principal civilized centers. I refer to infectious diseases and their differentiated incidence as between civilized and uncivilized populations.

Exposure to crowd diseases was one of the costs of civilization. Wherever large numbers of human beings clustered together, whether in cities and armies, on pilgrimage, or at fairs, disease organisms were capable of feasting themselves on the fair field of folk spread so invitingly before them, and did so almost from the start of civilized history. Small, isolated communities were incapable of sustaining diseases like smallpox and measles, which provoke long-lasting immune reactions in those who survive infection. Only the continual presence of a sufficient number of newborn and therefore vulnerable individuals could supply new human hosts indefinitely, maintaining a chain of infection from one susceptible person to another. This, in turn, required large populations in close enough touch to allow the virus a statistical chance of making a successful transfer from one infected person to a susceptible new host uninterruptedly, year in and year out. In such circumstances, children were most at risk; and these distinctively civilized infections became, in fact, the familiar roster of childhood diseases that circulated in my own youth but which have now, for the most part, been suppressed or eliminated by inoculation and other forms of medical intervention. Other diseases, especially those propagated by contamination of drinking water and food, also concentrated where human population was densest, that is, in cities, and in the rural areas most closely in contact with cities.

Important demographic consequences flowed from these disease patterns. Until after the middle of the nineteenth century, for example, cities were incapable of sustaining themselves demographically for very long without an influx of newcomers from the countryside. When endemic diseases did not regularly kill off more children than were born within the city itself, epidemics came at irregular intervals to cut back city populations drastically. Urban mortality rates of fifteen to as much as fifty percent in an epidemic year were matter of course in early modern times; and when such events became rare, after the seventeenth century, it was because intensified communication and larger urban concentrations of population invited endemic disease to settle in, creating a more nearly uniform shortfall of urban births over deaths. Rural communities could suffer epidemic too, of course, but exposure was greater in town because human contacts were more various and contaminated food and water affected larger numbers.

The disease vulnerability of urban populations before doctors learned how to control infections meant that cities required a flow of people as well as of food from afar in order to sustain themselves. The stability of civilized society therefore required that urban die-off be countered by population growth somewhere in the accessible countryside. Exact balance was scarcely to be expected; and in fact ancient and medieval cities suffered from periodic population shortages, just as they also suffered from famines. The standard response to an inadequate spontaneous reinforcement of the urban work force was forcible recruitment, i.e., enslavement. And, as Karl Marx pointed out more than a century ago, slavery bulked large in ancient times. As far as western Europe was concerned, slavery was modified into serfdom in late antiquity when population decreased drastically so that urban skills and the social differentiation based on diversity of skills almost disappeared.

In other parts of the civilized world, slavery continued to be important as a way of filling occupational niches for which there was an inadequate spontaneous supply. Sometimes, too, enslavement became a path to privileged social position, particularly for those who served in royal households and gained the confidence of kings and emperors. Moslem governments, alienated from their subjects by religious and other differences, regularly employed royal bodyguards of slaves from the tenth Christian century onwards. These strategically situated companies of armed slaves were often able to take power from rulers who feared their subjects so much as to need a slave bodyguard in the first place. The result was a series of slave dynasties, of which the most famous was the Mamluk regime in Egypt that lasted until 1798.

But whether slaves were drudges and outcasts at the very bottom of society or wielders of governing power and privilege, individuals qualified for their career as slaves only by becoming aliens and strangers in a new social setting. Detachment from inherited social ties was, indeed, the diagnostic trait of slavery; and uprooted slaves were usually denied a new social setting within which they could hope to reproduce themselves biologically. Slave populations therefore required constant reinforcement from afar. Plantation slavery of eighteenth- and nineteenth-century American history was unusual inasmuch as the Black slaves did reproduce themselves and actually increased in numbers almost as rapidly as the free population. But demographic growth rates in colonial times in temperate North America were altogether extraordinary, and should not be taken as a norm, whether for slaves or free men.

My point in this: ancient, medieval, and early modern disease patterns were such as to require cities to import labor; and in many instances, when spontaneous immigration from the nearby countryside proved insufficient, resort to enslavement supplied the shortfall, moving across wider cultural boundaries and greater distances to bring an unfree labor force into action. The result, needless to say, was ethnic mixture and pluralism on a grand scale in major centers of imperial government, and less complex mixing in provincial urban centers whose catchment area for immigrant labor was smaller and less variegated than the catchment areas needed to sustain imperial capitals.

Only in remote and barbarous lands did ethnic homogeneity prevail. Migratory tribesmen and other uncivilized communities could indeed maintain the simplicity and solidarity of society that allowed rulers and ruled to belong to the same cultural and biological community. Yet even in such communities, strangers sometimes intruded, perhaps only as temporary sojourners, tempting local taste with strange and exotic trade goods and showing what human skill and effort could achieve.

This points to a third factor in civilized life that assured ethnic mingling: the exchange of goods across cultural boundaries through some sort of organized trade. Valued goods originating in identifiable localities – items like obsidian flakes from the Aegean island of Melos or the native copper from Lake Superior's shores – traveled very long distances in prehistoric times, though exactly how they moved from hand to hand is unknown. When written records begin to cast new light, long-distance trade had already become a specialized occupation; a find of merchants' records from Asia Minor shows that laws and customs for the conduct of caravan trade were already well developed as early as the nineteenth century BC in the ancient Near East.

But in proportion as the import of goods became

part of everday activity, another kind of social and cultural mixing of peoples became normal and necessary. Merchants coming from afar were liable to linger, at least until they could accumulate a suitable return cargo; and some set up permanent residence to act as agents for their fellows and/or to perform other specialized services within the host community. Long-distance trade therefore gave birth to permanent communities of aliens in major urban centers. These trade and skill diasporas, like ancient slavery, attained legal definition from very early times, as the rights of merchants prescribed by the laws of Hammurabi show.

Centuries later, beginning about 500 BC, the rise of portable and universal religions – i.e., Buddhism, Judaism, Christianity, and Islam together with some less successful faiths like Manicheanism – provided an effective cultural carapace for trade diasporas, insulating them from their surroundings in matters of faith and family as never before. Portable and universal faiths, in fact, permitted followers of a religion that differed from that prevailing in the environing society to maintain a corporate identity indefinitely, generation after generation. The Jewish ghettoes of western Europe illustrate this possibility, in contrast to such a group as the Lombards, who gave their name to medieval London's financial center, but in the long run failed to maintain a separate existence in a society whose religion they shared.

In the most active and ancient centers of Eurasian civilization, i.e., in the Middle East and immediately adjacent regions, therefore, mingling of diverse peoples in urban centers through conquest, through enslavement, and through long-distance trade resulted in the creation of a series of social niches inhabited by one or another ethnic group. Such groups entered into conventional and relatively well-defined relations with one another, in accordance with a peck order of social prestige and deference. Upheavals in such arrangements occurred whenever a new conquest took place, and other shocks – for example, the rise of a new religious movement such as that associated with the name of Sabbatai Sevi among the Jews of the Ottoman empire in the seventeenth century – could alter ethnic alignments and balances rather abruptly. But in normal times, between such bouts of change, governments presided over an ordered ethnic diversity, and no one supposed that uniformity was desirable or that assimilation to a common style of life or pattern of culture was either normal or possible.

Further away from the Middle Eastern center the ethnic intermingling and complexity of human groupings lessened; and one can find some close analogues to the nation-state of modern times in sufficiently remote or marginal places. Japan, for example, was never successfully invaded by outsiders after the ancestors of the Japanese people established themselves on those islands in prehistoric times. Whatever ethnic diversity initially existed among those ancestors disappeared before historic records begin, save always for the gulf that separated the Japanese from the Ainu, whose share of the islands was gradually pushed back to the marginal northernmost parts of the archipelago. Chinese and Korean high culture came to Japan in due season, borne partly by Buddhist missionaries. But the Japanese quickly took the initiative in importing civilized skills and knowledge from the mainland, so that few foreigners ever found lodgment in the islands. To be sure, a handful of skilled Korean potters preserved a separate existence for centuries, and Japanese seamen may have brought some slaves into the country. But, in general, the Japanese preserved their ethnic homogeneity by defeating even the most formidable invaders, like Kublai Khan's Mongols, and by choosing for themselves what to admit to their homeland and what to reject or repel.

Japan's prickly autonomy and comparative isolation were well illustrated by the reception accorded European missionaries and traders in the sixteenth century. Initially, the newcomers were welcomed, conversion to Christianity became fashionable in some circles, and European guns were both admired and imitated with extraordinary success. But when European connections that went along with Roman Catholicism threatened to affect the political loyalties of a portion of the Japanese people, the central government ruthlessly repressed the new faith and drove out resident Europeans, cutting the Japanese off from the rest of the world almost completely.

More than any other civilized land, therefore, the Japanese islands maintained ethnic and cultural homogeneity throughout their history and at least in principle constituted a nation-state under the suzereignty of the emperor, even in ages of political fragmentation when military power and command rested in practice with clan leaders and their bands of sword-wielding samurai.

Unlike Japan, China was subject to recurrent conquest from the steppes, and Chinese settlers, as they penetrated southward from the initial core region of the Yellow River valley, engulfed a great number of other peoples who did not at once merge into the Chinese body social as undifferentiated subjects of the emperor. Moreover, in China's imperial eras, from the time of the Han dynasty onwards (202 BC to 220 AD), professional armies extended the emperor's political jurisdiction into central Asia and other borderlands, where an enormous diversity of peoples – Turks, Tibetans, Mongols, Manchus, Koreans, to name only those familiar to westerners – shared subjection with the Chinese to the dictates of a distant court.

China, therefore, did not retain anything like the isolation and ethnic homogeneity that characterized Japanese society. Willy-nilly, it belonged to the great Eurasian ecumene, subject to all the stresses and strains of living in uncomfortable proximity to peoples of different language, culture, and skills. Political and ethnic boundaries never coincided exactly. Instead, Chinese conquest of borderlands alternated with con-quest of part or all of China by peoples coming from those same borderlands.

Yet there is a sense in which Chinese civilization did attain and maintain a far greater cohesion than was true of civilizations in Europe, western Asia, and India. This resulted from the way Confucianism became institutionalized. Admission to the Chinese managerial elite came to depend less on inherited status than on mastery of the Confucian classics and of the style of life and thought they inculcated. This allowed persons of diverse background to become fully and completely Chinese simply by becoming learned. From about the tenth century AD suitably educated mandarins staffed the government, managed the court, and dominated society. Even Genghis Khan's heirs found the services of Confucian administrators indis-pensable. As a result, in 1368, when Chinese rebels successfully overthrew what the educated classes firmly felt to be an alien, barbarian regime, and brought a new native-born dynasty, the Ming, to power, any lingering foreign taint imposed upon China during the Mongol era was systematically repudiated and suppressed in the name of a restored and purified Confucian orthodoxy.

But this should not disguise from us the fact that earlier in China's long history far greater openness to innovation coming from the west had prevailed. The reception of Buddhism is, of course, the great monument to China's earlier readiness to borrow from abroad; and with Buddhism came a variety of secular changes like the enlarged scope for commerce and some technical skills and ideas (e.g. monumental sculpture) that remained central to later Chinese civilization.

The truth of the matter, it seems to me, is this: until about 1000 AD, China was ready and willing to learn from foreigners whenever they had anything worthwhile to teach because, up to that time, China's level of skills and attainment was no greater than that of other civilized communities. But between about 1000 and, say, 1450, China did spurt ahead and surpass the rest of the world in wealth, skill, and population. Marco Polo's awed account of the wonders of Cathay shows how a traveled and sophisticated European reacted to Chinese accomplishments in the late thirteenth century. A few decades later, Ibn Battuta's more cursory report of what he saw in China records a similar reaction, though China's complete indifference to Islam depressed that learned and pious Moslem traveler.

These experienced foreigners' reaction to Chinese wealth and skills lets us understand better how the

Chinese educated classes, accustomed after about 1000 to finding only inferiors outside Chinese borders, were deeply offended by the Mongol conquest, so that when the barbarian yoke was thrown off in 1368 the liberated Chinese elites were intent above all on keeping foreigners at arm's length. Looking backward was more comfortable than looking outward, even after a new barbarian dynasty, the Manchu, subjugated China in the mid-seventeenth century. The resulting defensive posture effectively insulated China from European probes in the early modern period after blunting imperial overseas explorations that might, under other circumstances, have led to a Chinese discovery of America on the one hand and of Europe on the other.

Such a history, I think, shows that the xenophobic unity of Chinese high culture in modern times was more a deliberate and exaggerated pose among the educated than a social reality. In fact, foreigners played an absolutely crucial role in China's history, even in those centuries when Chinese rulers and thinkers were most eager to repudiate them. Both Ming and Manchu dynasties actually presided over a multinational empire in which the numerical superiority of the massed Chinese peasantry supported a Confucian governing elite without itself entirely belonging to that privileged world.

Indeed, local dialects and ways of life varied substantially even within China proper, making the Chinese less like a single European nation than like the Latin (or Germanic) peoples of Europe – i.e., culturally and linguistically akin, but diverse enough in language and custom to constitute separate nationalities. If the papal monarchy had prevailed in medieval Europe, and been able to keep the German and Latin nations under a single overarching administration, entrusting government to clerics, trained in church law and using Latin for administrative purposes, the Chinese pattern of imperial unity would have been nearly replicated at the other end of the ecumene; but of course that was not how things turned out in the Far West.

Turning attention to that other flank of the Eurasian ecumene, I must confess that my vision of the past differs a good deal from the received version of classical and medieval history, affected as that was and is by nineteenth-century nationalistic notions and preconceptions. Somehow, we fasten attention on the privileged citizen body of Athens and Rome, forgetting the foreigners and slaves who also lived in those cities in their days of imperial greatness. Similarly, the royal Plantagenets are commonly considered English, even though they spoke Norman French and claimed suzerainty over more of France than the French kings did before King John lost out to his Capetian rival, King Philip Augustus, between 1202 and 1214. But if we try to escape such lopsidedness, so far as I can see the history of the ancient Mediterranean lands and of medieval Europe conformed quite closely to the polyethnic pattern that prevailed in the Middle East and in India from the very beginning of civilized society.

Classical city-states, to be sure, began as military and religious associations among ethnically homogeneous farming folk, and for varying lengths of time even victorious and expanding polities like those of Sparta, Athens, and Rome retained their predominantly rural, homogeneous character. But when politically successful classical city-states evolved into cities in the social and economic sense, concentrating comparatively large numbers of human beings within their walls while simultaneously maintaining contacts with distant places and peoples, the disease consequences of urbanism begin to assert themselves; and as that happened, the supply of citizen soldiers, whose expanding numbers had provided the basis for early political successes, dwindled and disappeared, giving way to an opposite demographic flow of slaves and foreigners into the new-sprung urban centers.

Sparta never made this transition; Athens did so in the fourth century BC and Rome in the second. But the greatest Athenian authors flourished while the transition from a homogeneous rural society was still underway; indeed their work was stimulated in large part by the strains and pains inherent in that transition. And the great Latin authors, who all date from Rome's imperial and urban age, looked backward to the pristine virtues of the early republic with such unanimity as to give that phase of Roman history a normative quality that moderns, affected by their own nationalist proclivities, tended to accept at face value.

Consequently, an idealized portrait of fellow citizens, sharing a common descent, a common culture, and above all a common public purpose in war and in peace, became central to the classical heritage of the western world. It was not entirely fictitious, for during a relatively short phase of both Athenian and Roman history a privileged corporation of citizens did indeed come close to such an ideal, and was able to maintain itself apart from those they conquered. But that exclusivity soon broke down, partly under the pressure of revolt among the subjected populations, and partly in face of demographic decay among the citizen body itself. Armed ventures overseas, and wars lasting for decades, were a sure way to kill off men of military age, through exposure to disease more than through exposure to enemy weapons. Only by gathering new manpower from beyond the boundaries of a single city-state could military conquest continue; and it was Rome's readiness to expand citizenship to an ever-widening circle of military recruits that assured its final victories.

Nothing much like a national state on the modern model emerges from such a history. The Kingdom of Macedon did, for a while, resemble European nation-states of the eighteenth and nineteenth centuries, since Macedonian expansion began from a broader territorial base than the city-states that had provided the initial political frame for Greek and Roman empire-building. But once the Macedonian kings were able, by importing Greek skills and training, to muster Macedonian manpower into phalanxes as efficient as those of the Greek cities to the southward, their success on every front transformed a national into a multi-national state within a single generation. Thus King Philip II (reigned 359–336 BC), starting from an almost purely Macedonian national base, ended his life presiding over a state that included Illyrians, Thracians, and Greeks as well as Macedonians; and his successor, Alexander (reigned 336–323 BC), accelerated the mixing of peoples under the Macedonian scepter with almost unimaginable rapidity. Macedonian history therefore exhibited a more rapid evolution from barbarian simplicity and cohesion to the ethnic pluralism characteristic of civilized polities than had occurred among the Greek city-states or was to occur in Italy.

The extraordinary prowess of Philip and Alexander together with the larger demographic base from which the Kingdom of Macedon started its imperial career made this precocious development possible. Indeed, the evanescence of Macedon's rural simplicity and barbarous ethnic unity is, or ought to be, a corrective to our proclivity to interpret ancient history in a nationalistic sense. And if Macedon is not enough, consider the Kingdom of David, which evolved from a confederation of Hebrew tribes into a polyethnic state within a single generation, for, as the Book of Kings tells us, David, an erstwhile shepherd boy, used the Jebusite city of Jerusalem as a base from which mighty men like Uriah the Hittite went forth to conquer peoples round about.

I conclude that ethnic homogeneity was indeed barbarous in the ancient Mediterranean world as well as in the ancient Orient, and regularly withered with the onset of civilized social complexity owing to the political, commercial, and epidemiological consequences of civilized social articulation.

Germanic, Iranian, and Turkish invaders, by trespassing on Roman imperial territory, inaugurated Europe's Middle Ages. East Rome survived to become the Byzantine Empire, and there polyethnicity along with authentic urbanity continued uninterruptedly from Constantine's age until 1453 and beyond. West Rome collapsed, giving way to Germanic kingdoms in which Germans and Latins lived uneasily together. Roman cities all but dissolved, owing partly to widespread depopulation and partly to the fact that Germanic landlords preferred to live in the country instead of gathering in towns as their Roman predecessors once had done. Simultaneously, regions beyond the Rhine and Danube evolved more complex social and political structures than those that had prevailed earlier in tribal society. In particular, professional warriors and Christian clerics achieved a separate status from ordinary cultivators; and kings, nobles, and clerics of the Germanic lands soon made room for increasing numbers of smiths, masons, shipbuilders, and other craftsmen. This pretty well closed the gap between the society of Mediterranean lands and the previously backward society of northern Europe. Indeed, by the tenth century if not before, the richer soils and more abundant rainfall allowed northwestern Europe to outstrip the Mediterranean in agricultural productivity, giving the north a new advantage.

The fundamental transformation was agricultural: the invention and spread of the moldboard plow and of the style of collective cultivation that best suited it. Long-acre fields with plow teams perpetually at work, except during the brief periods of seedtime, harvest, and the hard Christmas frosts, provided northwestern Europe with a new and much more productive husbandry, transforming the dank forests of Roman Britain and of ancient Germany into the open fields of medieval manors. When this transformation began is unsure – perhaps as early as the beginning of the Christian era – but it took many centuries to come anywhere near to completion. Only after about 900 AD did the new agricultural productivity of northwestern Europe begin to support the growth of towns and reinvigorate all the other expressions of civilization which had sunk very low during the Dark Ages of early medieval times.

Among those expressions, of course, was the rise of what we are accustomed to think of as national states: France and England, along with a fringe of others – Denmark, Sweden, Hungary, Poland, and perhaps Portugal as well. If one contemplates the geographical distribution of this list of 'national' states it is obvious that most of them were marginal to the main centers of Latin Christendom in somewhat the same way that Macedon had been marginal to the world of the Greek city-states before the time of King Philip. The great exception was the kingdom of France; but it was also not united in anything but name before 1202. Even after that date the authority of the royal government remained unstable until the French monarchy's eventual victory in the Hundred Years' War (1337–1453) finally separated the kingdoms of France and England from their previous embrace.

Until 1453, therefore, Latin Christendom, like classical Mediterranean society, was not organized along national lines in anything but name. Even the marginal kingdoms of Denmark, Sweden, Poland, and Hungary were not strictly national, since foreigners played critical roles in sustaining the royal power, acting as privileged traders and taxpayers, if nothing else. And in the most active centers of civilized life, that is, in Italy and the Low Countries, nothing resembling national structures existed. Instead, city-states consolidated their authority against rurally based rival lords of whatever rank and degree in the feudal hierarchy; while within city walls, immigrants from far and near were welcomed in accordance with the famous dictum 'Stadt luft macht frei.' Most newcomers came from close by and assimilated the language and culture of local urban elites swiftly and unobtrusively. Only a handful of Jews and some long-distance traders maintained their alienness, usually setting themselves up in special districts of the city.

The idea that government and people ought to share

common concerns was affirmed by a handful of civic humanists, who were inspired by classical models. They first voiced the notion in Italy in the fourteenth century. But this was initially an exotic and implausible notion. Christians knew full well that government came from God, mediated perhaps through the pope or emperor or both – or perhaps not. Kings and lesser rulers might have to coordinate their actions with the wishes of their principal military subordinates. King John's ill-fated career illustrated the cost of disregarding that elementary precaution. Taxpayers, too, might have to be consulted before cash could safely be collected from the handful of merchants and other urban dwellers who had enough money in their possession to be worthwhile objects of royal or princely taxation. Finally, bishops and other prelates of the church had to be conciliated, because their jurisdiction over the faithful competed with secular government, and in cases of collision, when ecclesiastical anger turned into anathema, even the boldest secular ruler had to hesitate, as King John's career also illustrated. But this fell far short of any sort of general partnership between rulers and ruled. Social and psychological gaps between nobles and commoners, burghers and villeins, rulers and subjects were too great to make the ideals of civic humanism seem sensible.

Nonetheless, the long-drawn-out struggle between the French and English monarchies that constituted the Hundred Years' War did, perhaps, give birth to the first stirrings of what grew into European nationalism in later centuries. The French peasantry – or some part thereof – learned to hate the 'goddamns' for their brutal ways; and English (or Welsh) mercenary soldiers reciprocated the dislike. Joan of Arc dramatized the collision; and Shakespeare later gave it lasting literary expression. Moreover, after 1453 the two rival kingdoms were separated by water, save for the residual English toehold at Calais; and as the two royal governments became stronger and reached downward to affect the everyday life of more and more persons, the city-state model of antiquity, as reformulated by Italian civic humanists, with its assumption of social solidarity between ruler and ruled, began to seem more plausible. That, at least, is one way to construe the political experience of modern Europe.

In my second lecture I propose to survey the rise of the idea of ethnic solidarity and the rightfulness of national independence. It is an utterly familiar story – *the* main theme of modern European history as worked out by my teachers and their predecessors. All I can or hope to do is to cast the familiar story in a somewhat new context, by bearing constantly in mind how eccentric and exceptional this idea and ideal were against the background of the human past as a whole.

## LECTURE TWO

**The Triumph of Nationalism, 1750–1920**

# The Triumph of
# Nationalism, 1750–1920

I
N MY FIRST lecture I of-
fered three reasons for the prevalence of polyethnicity
in civilized societies before 1750, arguing that conquest,
disease, and trade all worked in that direction, most
pronouncedly in the Middle East and somewhat less
forcefully towards the extremities of the Eurasian
ecumene. There ethnic diversity diminished, though
even in remote offshore islands, like medieval Japan
and Britain, aliens played significant roles as bearers
of special skills.

If my argument is sound, something must have
happened in western Europe about 1750 to alter
prevailing patterns of civilized society, since, as everyone knows, after 1789 the revolutionary government
of France made good a claim to the equal loyalty of
all inhabitants of the territory over which it ruled,
claiming that French citizens constituted a single

nation, with the right and duty of participating in public affairs. The consequences were considerable, not least of which was a quantum leap in the effective power of a government able to draft entire age classes of young men for military service in defense of the *patrie*. France's revolutionary success impelled other European governments to remodel themselves on a nationalist base insofar as possible. Revolutionary movements embraced the same ideal in those parts of Europe where rulers could not or would not accept nationalist principles. Nor was the idea long confined to Europe since, before the close of the nineteenth century, the nationalist idea of claiming rightful sovereignty for 'the people,' i.e., for those who shared a common ethnic heritage, had taken root in such distant places as India and China.

The triumph of nationalism is a familiar story: *the* central reality of modern times according to a notable company of academic historians who, first in Germany and then elsewhere, began to look for meaning in the historical record of the postclassical ages. They started their search in the aftermath of the revolutionary and Napoleonic wars that had so clearly demonstrated the superior power of the free, equal, and fraternal French nation-state. We are now living in the aftermath of another set of world-destroying and world-creating wars, and I shall argue that the wars of 1914–45 augured the eclipse of nationalism and of ethnic homogeneity within separate polities as clearly as the wars of 1792–1815 had announced the triumph of the principle of nationality and of an assumed ethnic homogeneity within separate sovereign states.

We are therefore able to see, as our predecessors were not, that the ideal of ethnic homogeneity within a particular geographic territory, and of national sovereignty conformable to ethnic boundaries, was time-bound and evanescent – inevitably so; a victim of its own success in much the same way that the classical ideal of a heroic and homogeneous citizenry also collapsed when first Athens, then Macedon, and finally Rome lived up to the ideal so successfully as to create an empire over others. Whereupon, as Horace and Juvenal make clear, the ruling ethnos began to suffer demographic decay, and so had to make room for slaves and subjects of diverse and different background merely to sustain the political and social structure its victories had erected.

To understand what happened in the eighteenth century to elevate the nationalist principle of according sovereignty to (presumptively) homogeneous ethnic groups, one must take due account of the heritage from the classical world that did so much to shape the minds of educated Europeans. In addition, new patterns of communication altered the boundaries of 'us' vs. 'them,' making standardized language far more important than it had been before. An extraordinary demographic surge likewise upset older social and economic patterns, setting everything in motion as new generations came of age but could not unthinkingly inherit the ways of life their parents had known because there were too many of them for preexisting occupational niches. Last but not least, military technology and organization made infantry the queen of battle and rewarded brute numbers on the battlefield in a fashion that has now, perhaps, passed away, along with so many other characteristics of the liberal, bourgeois age our grandfathers and great-grandfathers supposed would last forever.

Let me expatiate briefly on each of these factors
that came together about 1750, sustaining the triumph
of nationalism and making ethnic homogeneity seem
normal and natural to Europeans in an age when their
victories overseas and the expansion of world commerce were actually mixing peoples more vigorously
than ever before.

Without the classical model I do not suppose that
modern European nationalism could have taken the
forms it did. But, of course, the classical ideal was
very much alive in the minds of Europe's elites from
the time of the Renaissance. As classical Latin and
Greek became the staple of schooling, the pagan
authors of Rome and Greece started to offer educated
Europeans an ideal of a life built around participation
in a self-governing city-state, composed of citizens who
elected magistrates, assembled to deliberate on matters
of public concern, and in time of war exhibited the
disciplined heroism of well-trained infantrymen in
battles against their neighbors, far and near.

For a long time, common sense held that such a
pattern of life only fitted a city that was small enough
for a single speaker's voice to be heard by all the citizens
when they assembled to deliberate on matters of public
importance. As such, it remained an ideal perhaps,
but an ideal of the past, unattainable in practice, and
all the more precious because it had irretrievably
vanished from the face of the earth. Livy and Tacitus
taught as much; and even the most civic-minded
moderns, however much they might be attracted to
the ancient ideal as a counter to existing patterns of
subordination to ecclesiastical and secular authorities,
did not really expect to restore Roman virtue and
republican institutions. Macchiavelli and a few others

may have toyed with the idea; but even in Florence, where a simulacrum of antiquity seemed most nearly attainable, sharp differences among the citizenry and professionalization of the military banished the ancient style of freedom and equality from the realm of the possible.

Nevertheless, in medieval and early modern times the towns of northwestern Europe did approximate closely enough to ancient city-states to reinforce the appeal of civic humanism. Towns arose in that part of the world after about 1000 AD amidst a swarming rural population. Consequently, towns recruited their lower classes from the nearby countryside, and even the ravages of the Black Death in the fourteenth century, severe though they were, did not suffice to upset that migratory flow. Nearly all of the strangers from afar who penetrated the remote Atlantic drainage area of Europe after about 1000 AD were Latin Christians, and as such did not seem totally alien or permanently unassimilable. Jews were expelled from France and England during the crusades, and royal licenses for their return never endured long enough to reestablish stable Jewish communities in those two countries before the seventeenth century.

The comparatively great ethnic homogeneity of French and English towns in medieval and early modern times depended on the fact that local skills had developed sufficiently by the eleventh century that at the time of their expulsion Jews and other cultural aliens had little to contribute to the still slenderly developed urban life of that part of the world. In other regions of Europe the situation was different, and far more complex ethnic juxtapositioning resulted. In Spain, for example, Moslems, Jews, and Christians mingled in the towns as well as in parts of the countryside before 1492. Jewish urban communities also flourished in central and eastern Europe, where urban skills were in drastically short supply at the time when the opening of the Baltic to an interregional trade in grain, timber, and other raw materials began to transform the economy and society of eastern Europe in the fourteenth century. Armenians added another ethnic strain of sporadic importance, while throughout the borderlands of the Ottoman, Hapsburg, and Muscovite empires, Orthodox and Latin Christians, like oil and water, met without much in the way of cultural mingling.

But what mattered for the later rise of nationalism was the pattern of town and rural life in France and England, where sufficient homogeneity between urban populations and the surrounding countryside was sustained between the eleventh and seventeenth centuries to make an extension of the ancient civic ideal of citizenship to the kingdom as a whole seem conceivable by the mid-eighteenth century. I can sum up, perhaps, by saying that northwestern Europe's marginality to the Mediterranean center of medieval urbanism was analogous to the marginality of Athens and Rome to more-developed centers of urban life during their classical transition from barbarous homogeneity to civilized polyethnicity. This recapitulation of processes of urbanization and commercialization made the fit between antiquity and modernity in northwestern Europe far closer than elsewhere, and eventually encouraged revolutionary reformers of the eighteenth century to try to revive Roman republican virtue in all its glory.

Those revolutionaries, of course, were building on

centuries of administrative centralization, the work of officials and soldiers who strove to consolidate royal absolutism in late medieval and early modern times. The Hundred Years' War (1337-1453) was critical here, for the upshot disentangled the French and English kingdoms from one another geographically, and endowed the French king with a standing army and a tax system capable of supporting an armed force that was clearly superior to any and all domestic rivals in peacetime. Nonetheless, challenges to royal absolutism did not disappear until after a final flare-up in the seventeenth century. But armed rebellion was decisively defeated in France with the suppression of the Fronde (1653); whereas in England, where absolutism had never taken firm root, a remarkably flexible parliamentary sovereignty emerged from the Civil Wars and Glorious Revolution of 1688.

As tax collectors, law courts, and other manifestations of central government reached down to affect the lives of more and more people in France and England, accompanying networks of communication also expanded their range, acting partly in harmony with and partly in opposition to the agents of political and administrative centralization. Market relations between town and country, and among merchants living in different towns, were perhaps the most important of these networks. By the eighteenth century even the poorest peasants living in remote and mountainous regions of France and England had become accustomed to selling at least a portion of their product in order to pay rents or taxes and be able to buy things they could not make for themselves. Local self-sufficiency was in retreat before the advantages of specialization and market exchange so persuasively analyzed by Adam Smith in 1776; and as families and individuals entered the economic exchange network, they also exposed themselves to town-based cultural systems of values and meanings. Local differences tended to weaken; commonality across longer distances increased.

A second network directly affected only the professional and educated classes who constituted the reading public. These groups became sufficiently numerous, nonetheless, to support the emergence of a secularized republic of letters in the seventeenth century that extended far beyond the borders of any one European state, and indeed reached across the Atlantic to affect American minds from the beginning of French and English settlement in the New World. Earlier, religion had dominated, dividing Europe along confessional lines from the time of the Reformation. Protestant efforts to make the Bible accessible to ordinary believers gave new impetus to standardizing the principal languages of western Europe and helped to demote Latin from its traditional primacy. Parisian French came close to substituting itself for Latin within the secular republic of letters that arose in the seventeenth century, but English, fortified by Shakespeare's rendering of the London dialect and by the magnificent cadences of the King James Bible, always rivaled French as a literary medium in the same way that the English government rivaled the French in the long series of wars, beginning in 1688 and ending in 1815, which some historians, with characteristic mathematical imprecision, have dubbed the second Hundred Years' War.

A standard language, intelligible across a spectrum of local dialects, and accessible to anyone with the help of a few years of elementary schooling, provided a powerful new basis for expanding and delimiting national boundaries and for communication within the national group so defined. Messages actually transmitted depended on circumstance no doubt; and as is well known, influential French writers, reflecting on the ill success that came to French arms in the middle of the eighteenth century, turned to political and social themes after 1750 in a spirit critical of the monarchy and its servants.

American revolutionaries who, with French help, successfully defied the military power of the British government (1776-83), added fuel to the fire, both by bankrupting the French government and by offering a convincing example of republican virtue in modern dress. Perhaps, after all, the ancient ideals of civic freedom and duty could be applied even to a country as large as France, by allowing citizens to express their political will through elected representatives, just as the British had been doing through their Parliament, and as the Americans proposed to do through Congress.

The peasant majority of France had little share in such discussion. The lower classes of the towns, and especially of Paris, were a more volatile population, living as they did in the midst of chronic underemployment and at the mercy of sporadic shortages of bread. I do not think that anyone really can say what their thoughts were like in the decades before the French Revolution brought them suddenly onto the stage of world history. How much they shared in the Enlightenment, and how much they maintained a cultural universe of their own, is, so far as my reading shows, an unanswered question.

What can be said about the lower classes is that their problems were directly connected with the remarkable population growth that set in from about 1750, not merely in France and England but across most or all of the civilized world, i.e., in China as well as in eastern and western Europe, among the Christian subjects of the Ottoman empire as well as the Amerindian subjects of the Spanish empire in the New World. Japan and India may have lagged in responding to the new conditions; but inference suggests that Africa's population also started to grow. Even in the absence of full information, however, we know enough to recognize that the eighteenth-century surge in population constituted a turning point in human history. It marks the modern age off from earlier times in a fundamental sense. Never before, so far as anyone can tell, did human numbers spurt upwards everywhere, or almost everywhere, at once. Indeed, the phenomenon perhaps registered the ecological unification of the earth through human agency. Regional and local differences did not disappear; but by the end of the eighteenth century all parts of the world had become closely enough linked to experience parallel stimuli and, more often than not, reacted along similar lines.

My emphasis on global commonality should not disguise the fact that historians have no agreed explanation for what happened, or why. Weather improved in northwestern Europe in the eighteenth century, assuring better harvests, but there is no reason to assume that climatic change was everywhere beneficent to agriculture, and we do not know for sure that it was global. A more plausible explanation points to the spread of American food crops. Maize, potatoes, peanuts, and sweet potatoes became important in many parts of the Old World in the course of the eighteenth century, and everywhere had the effect of increasing the output of calories per acre of cultivated ground. Without their availability it is hard to believe that human populations could have grown as they did. But the new crops required more work in the fields than was needed to raise the crops they displaced, so the spread of American food crops may have reflected the population surge, not caused it.

My own effort at explanation emphasized the altered exposure to infectious diseases occasioned by the new permeability of the world's oceans to constant human movement. Diseases traveled with ships' crews unceasingly from port to port. Consequently, even landlocked populations, in touch with the ports through intensified commerce, suffered a shift from epidemic to endemic exposure. This put young children everywhere at risk, but insulated adults from the lethal effect of diseases like smallpox, whose epidemic visitations had previously constituted a major check on population growth. Young children continued to die of course, and perhaps in greater numbers than before. But they could be quickly replaced without breaking up families or interrupting work in the fields, as happened whenever adults of breeding age were exposed to epidemics.

Changes in age of marriage and deliberate efforts at regulating births may have mattered in some parts of the world as well. The complexities surrounding human reproduction and nurture are such as to make any simple and dogmatic explanation of what happened in the eighteenth century inadequate to the facts – many of which are unknowable, and sure to remain so.

Still, for my purposes here there are two obvious consequences of the new demographic balance. First of all, European cities had no difficulty in finding migrants from the surrounding countryside to replace the die-off that continued to prevail in disease-saturated urban environments. Thus even great cities like London and Paris could maintain an approximation to ethnic homogeneity, as before, in spite of exposure to infections of an intensity that in earlier ages had required recruitment from afar and among ethnically diverse populations. Consequently, rural newcomers continued to have no great difficulty in mastering Parisian French or London English, and, as Boswell may remind us, even Scotsmen could make themselves understood in eighteenth-century London, though not without consciously shaping their speech to conform to the conventions of the south.

The other obvious consequence of the population surge of the eighteenth century was that wherever uncultivated land was not readily available, rural populations faced a difficult choice as more children came of age than were needed to cultivate existing fields in accustomed ways. Generally speaking, this crowded condition prevailed west of the Elbe and north of the Pyrenees. In Spain and eastward of the Elbe, substantial amounts of uncultivated land awaited the plow when the population spurt started, so population pressure did not become important until sometime in the nineteenth century. But in France, Britain, the Low Countries, western Germany, and northern Italy the problem of too many sons and daughters coming of age for existing village niches was felt well before the century ended. Difficulties in the villages provoked discontent and desperation that reached to the bottom of society, constituting an essential background for the revolutionary upheavals of the years 1789–1815.

The fact that, by the later decades of the eighteenth century, familiar routines of life had become impossible for hundreds of thousands of young people in rural France and England meant that radical, new ideas about what was wrong with society acquired a resonance among the lower classes that could not have occurred otherwise. Revolutionaries, in other words, had a ready-made audience awaiting a call to action. Paradoxically, rural discontent found its most significant expression in towns and cities. There youthful migrants, seeking escape from an impossible situation in the villages, entered an overcrowded labor market in which their low skills condemned them to lifelong marginality. The Paris crowds that played so great a role in the heroic days of the French Revolution probably got their best fighting manpower from the resulting pool of underemployed malcontents.

In 1780, London crowds, facing equivalent difficulties, had turned their anger in a conservative direction by opposing Catholic emancipation and, not incidentally, attacking Irish immigrants who threatened to undercut their already straitened level of life. But the agitation surrounding John Wilkes, both before and after the Gordon riots of 1780, showed how easily the tide of discontent might have turned in a revolutionary direction if the interplay of personalities and political controversy had been such as to trigger a different crowd behavior.

To be sure, industrial and commercial expansion,

supplemented by emigration overseas, did, precariously, accommodate Britain's runaway population growth after 1750, while France took the path of political revolution. But the French had much to do with what happened offshore, once the national interest and honor of Great Britain came to be firmly associated with rejection of the newfangled slogans of liberty, equality, and fraternity emanating from across the Channel.

Ireland followed a different path, for that island met the population surge by large-scale conversion of pasturelands to grain fields between 1780 and 1815, responding to new markets that Britain's rising population created. The crunch between an expanding rural population and available land did not become unbearable until the 1840s, thanks to the fact that potatoes assured a minimal subsistence to a whole family from no more than two or three acres of land. The Irish experience prior to 1845 therefore corresponded to what happened east of the Elbe, where breaking new land to the plow, and widespread resort to potatoes (in the south to maize), allowed peasant communities to increase their numbers without altering old modes of life very significantly until sometime in the nineteenth century when land susceptible to conversion from pasture started to run out.

Reaction to the revolutionary promises proclaimed from Paris after 1791 reflected these conditions. Only where rural crowding had reached critical levels was there enough tinder concentrated in towns and cities to sustain a politically powerful response to the new republicanism. Elsewhere circumstances allowed only small revolutionary cliques to form without significant followings. Consequently, in trans-Elbian Europe, kings and officials of the Old Regime had little difficulty in maintaining a traditional style of leadership until such time as crisis on the land did develop. Then, and only then, did nationalist and (later) socialist ideas acquire the resonance that made them such powerful movements in the second half of the nineteenth century – in Ireland as well as in eastern Europe.

The fourth factor sustaining western Europe's atavistic political response to the modern age was military, echoing without really duplicating the military reality that had undergirded ancient city-states of the classical age. The central experience of citizenship in Athens, Sparta, and Rome hinged on participation in the armed forces. In an age when infantry dominated the battle-field, this meant long hours of training, learning to move in unison and keep formation. The effect of such drill on human psyches is very powerful, for it arouses the most elemental level of human sociability. In all probability, even before our remote ancestors could speak articulately, they danced, moving their limbs in unison and miming routines of the hunt. Sentiments of solidarity with one's fellows, of pride in personal and collective prowess, and a visceral sense of animal well-being still stream towards consciousness when fully articulate modern descendants of protohuman hunters imitate their ancestors by moving their limbs in unison while engaging in military drill. All modern armies depend upon being able to generate an entirely subrational comradeship among new recruits simply by marching about on a parade ground.

The peculiar intensity of political attachment that characterized Greeks and Romans in the heroic phase of their history fed on this phenomenon. Long hours of drill were required of young men before they could be safely counted on to keep their place in phalanx and cohort in the face of the enemy; and the graduates of such drill felt that they belonged to one another and to the city they embodied far more intensely than populations lacking such a bonding experience. That was the reason why Greek, Macedonian, and Roman troops so often triumphed over larger, less coherent barbarian armies. Drill, and the psychological residue it left behind, was indeed the principal secret of their imperial success – success, which, as I have said, undermined its own social basis.

At the very end of the sixteenth century, Maurice of Nassau, Stadthalter of Holland and of various other provinces in the Low Countries, deliberately revived Roman imperial practice, regularizing and intensifying infantry drill, and adjusting it to the employment of firearms. Results were spectacular and spread swiftly to other European armies in the course of the first half of the seventeenth century. The eager acceptance of Prince Maurice's style of military management, even as far afield as Muscovy, was promoted by the further fact that prolonged and repeated drill effectually dissipated the risks of inviting revolution by entrusting decisive military force to infantrymen, even when they were recruited from the humblest levels of society. The experience of drill reliably transformed outcasts of society into obedient soldiers, ready and willing to risk life and limb in response to words of command shouted at them by their officers. Ties to civil society almost ceased to matter since well-drilled soldiers' fellow feeling concentrated upon their companions in the ranks. Fed, clothed, and disciplined by duly accredited agents of constituted political authorities, they could afford to forget civil society, and did.

This was a very important change, because it allowed European rulers freely to exploit the efficacity of handguns for the first time. In earlier centuries, European princes could not afford to trust infantry fully. Commoners, armed and organized to fight on foot, were chronically liable to challenge their social superiors. The revolutionary possibilities inherent in this situation had been familiar ever since Italian and Swiss footsoldiers had shown the way by defeating nobly born knights in the battles of Legnano (1126) and Mortgarten (1315). But after Maurice of Nassau's reforms, infantry formations lost their revolutionary potential. Political authorities, embedded in an existing hierarchy of classes, could feel perfectly safe in relying on 'the scum of the earth,' as Wellington once called his soldiers, to defend and expand royal and princely domains, at home and overseas.

Even the best-drilled soldiers needed food, clothing, weapons, and pay; and governments needed tax income to provide these essentials. These needs supported and confirmed the alliance, dating back to the Middle Ages, between town-based capitalists and merchants on the one hand and royal or princely authority on the other. By protecting the exchange economy, and collecting money taxes from its principal beneficiaries, political rulers could afford to maintain efficient armies and thereby maintain or, in favorable situations, even expand their power. And between the seventeenth and twentieth centuries, an efficient army meant the predominance of infantry, the more numerous and more rigorously drilled the better.

The possibility of expanding state power by combining military training with the duties of citizenship had occurred to reform-minded French officers even before the Revolution so it was not entirely a stab in the dark when the convention, in 1793, summoned all Frenchmen to the defense of the *patrie* through the famous *Levée en masse*. Manpower abounded, Roman precedents pointed in that direction, and training cadres were available from the royal army. As a result, modern drill, supplemented by revolutionary ideology, swiftly worked its magic on the recruits, making them obedient, efficient soldiers, no matter where they came from or what their political or social ideas may have been before they found themselves in the ranks. This social-psychological phenomenon assured the success of the revolution, and, incidentally, provided a new outlet for surplus rural numbers, thereby relieving the problem of too many hands for available jobs that had troubled the last days of the Old Regime.

Revolutionary French power, of course, soon reached far beyond the borders of the kingdom and transcended the limits of the French nation. Towards the end of his career, Napoleon's armies drew manpower from Germany, Italy, and the Low Countries as well as from Poland. Such recruits were quite as loyal and obedient as those coming from France proper. Yet the capacities of military drill and Napoleonic administration to meld diverse nationalities into a single imperial command did not prevent France from reenacting the antique political pattern whereby military success turned a putative community of brothers into a tyranny over others. This transmutation had become apparent in Spain and Prussia even before the invasion of Russia in 1812 provoked the paroxysm of anti-French feeling in Russia, Germany, and Britain that finally overthrew Napoleon.

Nevertheless, between 1792 and 1815 the power

attained by the French nation dazzled all of Europe, and made adaptation of the political practice that sustained such power a matter of urgency for other European governments. Accordingly, partnership between people and rulers, more intimate and extended than had ever seemed feasible before, became the political agendum of the nineteenth century. Shared national identity, on the French model, seemed the key. Greatness awaited peoples who could act together as brothers in harmony with one another and with their government, while weakness and ignominy threatened rulers so alienated from their people as to remain incapable of winning unstinted popular support. From an upper-class point of view, revolutionary liberty and equality were too high a price to pay for fraternity; but in the second half of the century Disraeli, Bismarck, and Russian Slavophils were able to show that nation-wide fraternity could accept and even reinforce existing social hierarchy.

After what I have said, I scarcely need to underline the extraordinary coincidences and synergies that came together in western Europe at the close of the eighteenth century to give birth to modern nationalism. Without the classical inheritance and a system of education built upon the classics, without the peculiarities of medieval town life in northwestern Europe, without intensified communciations playing upon a powerful surge of population growth, and without a military system that rewarded mass mobilization of the citizenry, modern nationalism could not have come into being, first in France and subsequently in other European countries. And, ironically, the failure of Napoleon's effort to build a transnational empire on the strength of an aroused and mobilized French nation assured the idea and practice of the ethnically unitary nation-state of rather more than a century of florescence. Eventually, the wars of 1914–45 undermined the political verities of the nineteenth century by revealing the all but unbearable costs of national rivalry within Europe, while simultaneously recapitulating Napoleon's imperial practice of transcending national boundaries for the more efficient conduct of hostilities.

Actually, the high costs of reorganizing society into ethnically uniform national units had been felt across much of the civilized world long before it began to haunt western Europeans in the twentieth century. Lands where polyethnic hierarchy had long prevailed, in accordance with the norms I analyzed in the first lecture, could not adjust to the atavistic pattern of modern nationalism without painful and disruptive civil strife, featuring local massacre of ethnic minorities. Islamic societies were especially at risk. The internal struggles that paralyzed and impoverished the Ottoman Empire in the nineteenth century constitute a classic example of the price to be paid whenever the will to acquire the talisman of national greatness was strong while the social context within which the idea had to be pursued was stubbornly refractory.

In India and China problems were less acute, largely because the contagion of European political ideas came more slowly and affected relatively few, even when, in the first decades of the twentieth century, Indian and Chinese nationalist movements did begin to affect the public peace. There was a second reason why the disruptive force of nationalism within a polyethnic context, so evident in Moslem countries, was less apparent in India and China. Potential internal frictions were initially obscured by the fact that the thrust of nationalist sentiment was directed against Europeans, who were ruling all of India and exercised far-reaching control over China, even though the trappings of sovereignty remained in Manchu hands until 1911. Consequently, anti-imperialist nationalism actually bridged linguistic and religious differences within India, which under other circumstances might have become radically divisive; while in China, the remote geographical location of the subject peoples of the empire meant that nationalist and revolutionary ideas, inspired from Europe, began their circulation among ethnic Chinese, principally among those who lived in coastal cities where the European presence was strongest.

In some countries, nationalist ideals of ethnic solidarity and shared destiny served to unite rather than divide. Germany and Italy in Europe, and Japan in Asia, were the important instances of this possibility; and the success that crowned efforts in each of these countries to establish a nation-state in the 1860s and 1870s seemed to prove the beneficence and practicality of the whole idea. The further fact that the United States survived its Civil War (1860–65), and continued to expand across the North American continent, affirmed the same principle. Other segments of the Great Frontier of European overseas settlement also started to consolidate into national states in the aftermath of such convincing demonstrations of the gains to be expected from political unity. Canadian Confederation and the political consolidation of Australia and South Africa were the principal instances of this effort.

Latin America constituted an intermediary case, for

in that part of the world nationalism had both divisive and unifying impact. Early in the nineteenth century, the imposing fabric of the Spanish empire broke up in face of nationalist and liberal revolt; and Brazil seceded from Portugal shortly thereafter. New nations, each different from its neighbor and often mutually hostile as well, emerged from the imperial fragments. Their consolidation presented challenges analogous to those faced within the countries of the British Commonwealth, with the difference that in the more tropical Latin American countries people of mixed blood, with Amerindian and African as well as European ancestors, constituted a large proportion of the population, and could not be denied political power.

Brazil and Mexico thus advertised to the world the sort of racial encounters which characterized all lands of European overseas settlement. In none of them did the notion of a single people, occupying a distinct territory, and therefore entitled to a sovereign national government all their own, correspond to reality. Polyethnic hierarchy prevailed in the 'new' lands in much the same fashion as it did in the ancient imperial societies of Asia, and for the same reason, since the dominant ethnic groups in old and new countries alike were in practice the descendants of conquerors. Relations among ethnic groups varied enormously, being defined by complex historic factors, including the balance of numbers among different peoples, and how inherited skills and traditions of the subordinated populations fitted into the skills and traditions of the dominant ethnic group.

Yet when I was young, these obvious facts were almost disregarded. The national ideal, as defined by France in its revolutionary era, prevailed even (or especially) in lands where ethnic pluralism contradicted the fundamental assumption of a uniform citizenry, bonded into nationwide brotherhood. Within the borders of France's historic rival, for example, English, Scots, Welsh and Irish nationalities shared the ground without dissolving into a single nation. Yet until the widespread enthusiasm for Irish independence became unmistakeable at the beginning of the twentieth century, Englishmen, at least, habitually spoke and acted as if all the inhabitants of the British Isles were a single people on the French model.

For that matter, France itself was never entirely French. Apart from German-speakers in Alsace-Lorraine, and Celtic speakers in Brittany, the gap between Langue d'oc and Langue d'oïl divided peasant France into significantly different communities. Indeed, one may argue that the incandescent quality of revolutionary propaganda in the crisis of 1793–4 was partly a deliberate effort to override such local divergences by insisting on the sacredness of the republic, one and indivisible.

Much the same might be said of other European nationalisms which papered over local differences of varying magnitude by virtue of the commonality of a school-learned language and whatever commonality of historical experience could be discovered or invented by industrious, nationalistic historians. In other cases, of course, commonalities of history were minimized or denied in order to separate an oppressed nationality from its oppressors – a tactic characteristic of revolutionary nationalists in Hapsburg and Ottoman lands, and of the Irish in Great Britain.

Obviously, human capacity to see what we wish to see and neglect awkward incongruities is very great;

and the national myths of the nineteenth century exercised that capacity to the full. The invisibility of French and Indians in the version of Canadian nationalism to which I was exposed in my youth was matched by similarly distorted self-images in other countries, not least in the United States of America, where ethnic unity was conveniently postponed to an indefinite future, i.e., until the melting pot had had enough time to do its work. Yet no one really thought that the melting pot would turn Blacks and Indians into simulacra of the Yankee version of Americanism, which was what it was supposed to make of European immigrants. Like Indians and Frenchmen in the Canada of my youth, these citizens of the United States were strangely invisible to the majority of their fellow Americans.

Yet the myth of national brotherhood and ethnic unity mattered. It justified sacrifice in war; it sustained public peace at home; it strengthened the hand of government in everyday affairs. No modern state could afford to be without it, as the hapless fumbling of Hapsburg, Ottoman, Romanov, and Chinese imperial regimes throughout the nineteenth century demonstrated. For more than a century after 1792, national unity, and a government responsive to the people, seemed the supreme secret of politics – the sure and attested way of attaining power and wealth. Only so could active partnership of people and rulers be sustained; and on this partnership, according to the liberal vision of history, all human greatness depended. No wonder our forefathers were intent on inventing a nation, one and indivisible, in which to take shelter, regardless of the social diversity and ethnic pluralism that actually prevailed!

## LECTURE THREE

Reassertion of the Polyethnic Norm since 1920

# Reassertion of the Polyethnic Norm since 1920

I

N THE LAST lecture I analyzed the strange case of national ethnic unity, a barbarous ideal, never perfectly realized in western Europe, yet enthusiastically embraced at exactly the time when western European nations were building world-girdling empires, where diverse peoples met and mingled on a scale never equaled before. The consequent polyethnic hierarchy in all the lands of European expansion contrasted sharply with the ideal of national unity that prevailed in the part of Europe most active in imperial venturing. Such an antithesis was intrinsically unstable, because the special conditions supporting the ideal and partial reality of national ethnic unity, discussed in my last lecture, were transitory, whereas the factors promoting ethnic mixing were enduring. They are indeed norms for civilized society, as argued in my first lecture.

The accelerated mingling of diverse peoples within state boundaries that we everywhere witness in our own time, and specifically since World War I, is therefore a return to normal as far as western European nations are concerned. It brings both gains and losses, as every important change inevitably does. My task today is to anatomize what has happened since about 1920 as incisively as our continuing immersion in the ongoing process allows.

World War I assuredly constituted a watershed, but its relationship to the ideal and practice of ethnic unity within national states was, to say the least, ambiguous. 'National self-determination' was one of President Wilson's Fourteen Points, ostensibly accepted by the victors as a basis for the peace. Russian Marxists also endorsed national self-determination, at least in matters cultural and linguistic, even though international proletarian solidarity, expressed and spearheaded by the Communist party, sought to bridge national barriers everywhere, or at least within the family of peoples constituting what soon came to be called the Union of Soviet Socialist Republics.

These ideological commitments attained a modicum of practical embodiment. Wilsonian principles were fleshed out in the form of a cluster of new nation-states in eastern Europe, although the complexities of ethnic distribution on the ground meant that important minorities continued to exist within the new boundaries – minorities which, in most cases, were unwilling to assimilate to the newly dominant nationality, whatever it might be: Pole, Czech, Serb, Rumanian, or Greek. Within the Bolsheviks' sphere of influence, likewise, new soviet socialist republics were delineated on the map, even though all important economic and political decisions continued to be made in party circles, and at the center in Moscow.

From the day of their birth, these tangible embodiments of the nineteenth-century ideal of encasing each ethnic group within its own separate state fell painfully short of expectations. Economic and other difficulties multiplied; ethnic and class frictions were scarcely diminished. Consequently, in central and southeastern Europe the liberal, nationalist recipe for public happiness soon turned sour in the mouths of all but a small clique of officials and politicians who staffed the new governments and profited from their new dignities and power. Revolutionary aspirations found new channels – Marxist, Fascist, Zionist, or old-fashioned eschatological as the case might be.

The Communist recipe likewise profited small ruling cliques, but ethnic groups within the Soviet Union differed markedly in the degree of disenchantment this fact generated among the rank and file. Some, the Armenians for example, remembering wartime massacres at the hands of the Turks, and, traditionally shrewd in all their dealings with the Russians, quite enjoyed their new autonomy, limited though it might be. Others, like the Tatars of Crimea, remembering a glorious past and unable to live up to it in the present, continued to sulk. A heavy-handed police regime so limited channels of communication as to inhibit overt expression of dissent; nothing comparable to the organized revolutionary movements of the rest of Europe (and the world) could therefore arise within Soviet borders, whether among the Great Russians themselves or among the various subject and associated nationalities of the Soviet Union. Yet this fact does not in itself prove that Lenin's nationalities policy met the needs and wishes of the population at large any better than watered-down Wilsonianism did in central and eastern Europe. After all, acute domestic friction, ostensibly based on social class – remember the liquidation of the kulaks – prevailed in Stalin's Russia as much or more than it did in the rest of interwar Europe.

The failure of national self-determination to solve social and political problems satisfactorily in the countries where it was tried after 1918 reinforced a spirit of postwar disillusionment that grew up among the victors. Many survivors concluded that if national sovereignty involved such mass slaughter as had been experienced in France in 1914–18, then the whole ideal was faulty, and ought to be rejected in favor of some sort of internationalism. The League of Nations was Wilson's answer of course; and a company of optimists, mainly living in Britain, the Commonwealth, and the United States, hoped that the conflicting claims of national sovereignty and world order might be effectively resolved through more or less public deliberative processes at Geneva.

A different tone prevailed in France, where fear of German revival was far stronger. There a group of tough-minded soldiers and politicians pinned their faith on preserving and expanding wartime transnational administrative devices that had been invented for the more efficient prosecution of the war, with the difference that since Britain and the United States were unreliable partners (and would not accept subordination to France anyway) their new partner should be Germany, or rather part thereof, i.e., the Rhineland or, better yet, the Rhineland and the Ruhr.

This recipe for the future transgressed national boundaries in the name of security for victorious France. It was backward looking, seeking to restore a situation like that of the age of Louis XIV and Napoleon, when a divided Germany allowed French diplomats and soldiers to dominate the European continent. Yet, it was also forward looking as events after World War II suffice to show. For the French agents who sought to detach the Rhineland from the rest of Germany and bind it to France with enduring economic and political ties anticipated the Iron and Coal community and the EEC in important ways. One of the key actors in the negotiations of the 1920s, Konrad Adenauer, lived long enough to play a leading role in the remarkable transnational reorganization of western Europe after World War II. Continuity in his ideas and outlook was real and to be expected; what changed was British and American reaction to transgression of the principle of national sovereignty as between France and (parts of) Germany. In the 1920s, Anglo-Americans opposed the French initiative and accounted it wickedly imperialistic; in the 1950s they accepted and supported transnational economic management as necessary for European prosperity and stability.

In the 1920s, the French experiment with transnational economic and political organization failed, owing to German, British, and American opposition, and in the following decade the League of Nations collapsed in the face of Japanese, Italian, and German defiance, compounded by lukewarm support from Great Britain and outright abandonment by the United States. Transnational administration for the more effective management of the war effort, which had been improvised during the conflict, was remembered only by a few economic experts and military men. Yet in a real sense, it was this dimension of World War I that presaged the eclipse of the ethnically unitary west European nation-state more authoritatively than did anything else.

The plain fact was that after the initial offensive in 1914 failed, the states of Europe, except for Russia, proved too small to fight a prolonged war solely on the strength of domestic resources. French dependence on Britain, and French and British dependence on the United States, even before American belligerency added military manpower to the balance, is well known. Germany, likewise, drew resources both from occupied countries in the west and from allied and subjugated lands in the east, mostly food and raw materials. The kaiser's Reich provided the Hapsburgs, Bulgaria, and Turkey with heavy weapons and other special services in return. However, the giant state of Russia, itself a multinational empire, had to rely almost wholly on its own resources; and the collapse in 1917 was accelerated by that fact.

But capacity to repel foreign rivals in war on the strength of domestic resources was one of the two critical criteria of sovereignty, the other being capacity to repress domestic revolt. European governments in World War I proved incapable of doing so. The increase in power attainable through transnational specialization and organization was too great, and the pay-off for systematic coordination of effort, on the battlefield and behind the lines, was too obvious to be foregone. Similar transnational organization had characterized the Napoleonic wars at their height, only to be repudiated and forgotten after 1815. The same seemed to have happened after 1918 with the collapse of the

Central Powers and the dismantlement of ad hoc administrative structures such as the Allied Maritime Transport Council and Supreme Military Command. If World War I had been followed by a century of peace, the parallel would have been complete, but in fact World War II came along twenty-one years later. As a result, in all belligerent lands veterans of the first conflict were still in positions of authority from which they swiftly reconstituted and then expanded the transnational administrative structures needed to fight efficiently.

Instead of stumbling into improvisation, forced upon them by stark necessity, as had happened in 1915–18, the Allied powers of World War II deliberately and consciously wove a transnational web for maximizing their war effort, from the initiation of hostilities to their close. First France and Britain, then Britain and the United States, then Britain, the US, and the USSR concerted strategic war plans and cooperated in adjusting the domestic production of goods of every kind to fit the ever-shifting requirements of future campaigns. New statistical data and concepts – what came to be called macroeconomics – gave hitherto unimagined precision to large-scale management of the war effort in Britain, Canada, and the United States; and Lend Lease allowed effective pooling of resources across national boundaries without financial restriction. The Soviet economy retained its prewar methods of management, and was only marginally integrated into the Anglo-American military-economic administrative structure. Nevertheless, supplies from outside powerfully assisted the Russian war effort, providing massive amounts of food and most of the trucks for the Red Army's last campaigns of the war.

The Japanese and Germans were notably less successful in concerting transnational mobilization. The ideological commitments of Tojo's Japan and of Hitler's Germany made cooperation with other nations on anything like an equal basis all but impossible. Compulsion could substitute, and did within Hitler's Europe; but Japan's efforts to establish a 'Co-Prosperity sphere' among Asian peoples liberated from European rule met with only limited success, owing, largely, to transport difficulties. Japan, nevertheless, ranks as principal gravedigger for the European empires of the Far East, and Hitler must be counted among the fathers of the EEC. It is indeed supremely ironical that a man who really believed in the racial unity and superiority of the German people, and who built his political career on such doctrines, should have presided over the forcible recruitment of millions of foreign laborers to work in Germany, while sending millions of Germans to fight, govern, and play the role of master in the countries from which the slave laborers came. Ethnic intermingling on a hitherto unexampled scale resulted – a perverse presage of things to come on a peacetime basis in the prosperous decades after the war.

Reaction, of course, set in after 1945. The German occupation forces fled, taking millions of *Volksdeutsch* with them. Most of the slave laborers went home. However, postwar flight and removal of persecuted and persecuting minorities prolonged the wartime ethnic mixing of the peoples of Europe into the immediate postwar years, and affected millions. Then, when economic recovery went into high gear, in the 1950s, a new current of migration asserted itself. Labor shortages in western Germany attracted new immigrants, first from east Germany then, when that source of supply was cut off by the erection of the Berlin Wall in 1961, from agriculturally backward regions of Europe, mainly the Mediterranean lands.

This restored a part of the wartime migration pattern within Europe; and in fact it was often persons who had worked in Germany during the war as slave laborers who were the first to go back from countries such as Greece and Yugoslavia. The millions of *Gastarbeiter* in Germany today are therefore direct successors to the wartime slave laborers. Hitler's involuntary betrayal of his principles of race purity therefore prepared the way for western Europe's postwar transnational economy, demonstrating how dramatically production could be increased by uprooting millions of ethnically diverse ex-peasants from the land and setting them to work in factories and mines and at other low-skilled urban occupations.

The Soviet Union had proved the same thing in its prewar Five Year plans, and continued to exploit the growth potentialities of shifting labor from agriculture to urban occupations in the postwar recovery period. This strategy lost its effectiveness when underemployed manpower in the Russian villages began to run out; and by the 1970s the Soviet economy, like that of the industrial states of western Europe, confronted a situation in which the principal remaining rural reserve of underemployed labor concentrated in culturally alien lands – in this case, in the Central Asian republics, where high birthrates continued to provide a copious supply of young people, whose Moslem heritage marked them off sharply from the Russians.

In western Europe, wartime exigencies were not the only forces at work in breaking down old ethnic and political boundaries. Among the factors that helped to bridge the antithesis between war and peace, and between Nazism and liberal political practice, one influential strand was French technocratic thinking. This vision of the possible had struggled towards expression between 1915 and 1925, been reduced to sectarianism during the 1930s, but had blossomed under Vichy both in governmental circles and, more significantly, in the ranks of the Resistance. French technocracy therefore survived the liberation and became one constituent of public debate over what had gone wrong in the interwar years and what should be done towards postwar reconstruction.

Catholic traditions of solidarity across national lines and Catholic doctrines of social justice were another key constituent of the postwar political scene. Moreover, the fact that a separated eastern Germany was solidly Protestant gave Catholic Germans of the Federal Republic a strategic opportunity they had lacked since Bismarck's time. Within western Germany, they could expect to neutralize the nineteenth-century Protestant predominance, since numbers matched one confession against the other about evenly. Accordingly, Konrad Adenauer and his successors stabilized the new religious geography by systematically interleaving Catholics with Protestants in the administrative hierarchies of the Federal German Republic.

Moreover, Adenauer and other German Catholics were prepared to cooperate with French politicians like Robert Schuman in a way that was inconceivable without their shared religious background. Indeed, in Schuman's case, a German name, Alsatian birth, and early nurture within the kaiser's Reich made close connection with Germany a kind of second nature, while the wartime experience of defeat and occupation convinced most of his fellow Frenchmen that national greatness could only be restored in association with the Germans by substituting French leadership for the detestable Nazi domination of western Europe. Most Germans, for their part, were eager to shed the opprobrium of Nazi crimes by becoming good Europeans.

A final factor in this constellation of circumstances was the American government's faith in free (or almost free) trade across political boundaries. Soviet autarky meant that such measures could not be applied globally, as American economists and policy-makers had hoped during the last years of the war. But at least they could be recommended to Europeans living within the American sphere of influence in western Europe. In his famous speech of June 1947, General Marshall added the bait of American aid for nations that would and could plan a European recovery program in common. That sufficed to tip the balance, and opened a way for economic cooperation across national boundaries within western Europe that has lasted ever since.

Among the barriers that disappeared in the postwar recovery period were legal obstacles to migration across national lines. As a result, not just in Germany but in all of the industrially developed west European lands, a sustained burst of prosperity in the 1950s and 1960s attracted millions of foreigners to low-paying, low-prestige jobs for which native-born workers were not available. But as European prosperity increased, foreign workers were recruited from further and further away, and became less and less assimilable to the host society.

The result was to create polyethnic hierarchies on European soil, analogous to similar hierarchies which had existed in European colonial empires before the wars, and in lands of European overseas settlement from the moment of initial immigration. Thus we can say that Europe's proudest nations were catching up with the rest of the world, willy-nilly – or sinking to its level, if one values ethnic unity and cultural cohesiveness more highly than wealth and power.

Among the world's leaders, only Japan remains inhabited exclusively by a single people, and has been able to profit from that fact in something the same fashion as the powers of western Europe profited from their domestic homogeneity (or near homogeneity) in the decades before 1914. Yet even in Japan, sharply falling birthrates forecast an end to rapid industrial and commercial expansion on the basis of an ethnically united work force.

What happened? What explains such a reversal of what once had seemed eternal verities? The question is perhaps better reversed by asking, as I did in my second lecture, what confluence of special factors sustained and fed ethnic unity in some parts of Europe in the late eighteenth and throughout the nineteenth century? For once we are conscious of those factors, it is easy to see how they have begun to weaken or disappear. In particular, ideas have altered, demography has altered, military organization has altered, and the continuing intensification of communications and transport, instead of favoring national consolidation, has begun to work in a contrary sense, inasmuch as its range transcends existing political and ethnic boundaries. Let me say a bit more about each of these changes.

First, ideas. Hitler's obsession with race and race

purity discredited one important aspect of earlier European notions about national unity and its importance. In particular, his genocidal campaign against Jews and Gypsies, together with his intention of exterminating Slavs standing in the way of German *Lebensraum*, aroused intense horror and repulsion when the gruesome facts about Nazi death camps became known. The effect in postwar decades was twofold. On the one hand, it tainted advocacy of the ideal of ethnic unity within an existing state, since such sentiments smacked too much of Nazi doctrines. On the other, Jews in particular, and other ethnic minorities subsequently, began to abandon the ideal of assimilation to locally prevailing national groups. What had happened in Germany seemed to prove its futility, for German Jews had practiced a policy of assimilation longer and more enthusiastically than had been tried in any other European country, with the possible exception of France! Even before the French revolutionaries made religion a private matter, and removed all legal obstacles to the assimilation of Jews, similar ideas had taken root in Germany's cultivated circles, as the friendship of Moses Mendelssohn (1729–86) with Gotthold Lessing (1729–81) may remind us. But if assimilation merely provoked brutal backlash in the heartlands of European civilization, what use to pursue it elsewhere? Was it not better to accept or even accentuate differences? Or was migration to Israel preferable? But, ironically, the new Jewish homeland, after its establishment in 1947, instead of resolving religious-ethnic tensions between Jews and others, as the founders of Zionism had hoped, actually intensified such frictions, and internationalized them by creating a Palestinian refugee population that refused to acquiesce in its expulsion from lands seized by the Jews.

Other, previously quiescent minorities also awoke to a new sense of permanent, collective identity in the postwar decades. Conspicuously, the Blacks in the United States did so; but the French in Canada, and Flemings in Belgium, together with a small company of noisy Scottish and Welsh nationalists in Great Britain, all moved along parallel paths. If national uniformity was not a good to be treasured, it was not worth striving for; and since such striving required erasure of distinguishing cultural differences, the spokesmen for subordinated ethnic groups could appeal to emotionally vibrant symbols – language above all, but also religion, folkways, costume, and the like. Such things, remembered from childhood, had a potential for arousing strong nostalgia among dwellers in large cities, whose daily encounters with individuals of differing cultural and ethnic backgrounds were impersonal and cool at best, and easily degenerated into abrasive collision.

Before 1914, in Europe and many other parts of the world as well, peasants and country bumpkins, looking to the city for models of a better life, had been willing and even eager to assimilate as best they could to a middle-class, city-based national norm in language and manners. But city folk, born and bred in the streets, needed what rural folk inherited automatically and unthinkingly: a primary group to belong to – or leave behind, but against which personal choices and career success could always be measured. In a perverse way, the Nazi hypertrophy of nationalism and race-feeling expressed this urban yearning for membership in a primary community. Reaction against its catastrophic consequences for Europe and the world simply redirected that yearning from the nation as a whole towards a variety of subnational groupings.

Demography reinforced and inflamed these new tides in the climate of opinion. A sharp decline of birthrates in Europe (including Russia), and in lands of European settlement overseas, was matched by sustained high birthrates in poorer lands, while improved medical services accelerated population growth, reducing deaths from infectious diseases very markedly. In the western world deliberate birth control allowed economic expectations to become more and more decisive in fixing the number and timing of births. Some Europeans had been influenced by such considerations for many centuries; but until the 1880s and 1890s deliberate limitation of births had not been sufficiently widespread (except in France) to have much demographic effect. This had meant that even the meanest and most marginal occupations could be filled readily enough by migrants from the crowded countryside nearby.

The effect of the two great wars of the twentieth century on this traditional pattern was drastic. New attitudes and ideas were widely propagated by the prolonged exposure of millions of men to military sex practices which dated back to Old Regime armies, and involved quite effective prevention of births. Women's experiences of wartime employment in factories and offices were probably even more significant. Marriage and motherhood no longer appeared as the only possibility; and even in those parts of eastern Europe where peasant life had persisted into the 1930s with little change, the drastic upheavals of World War II broke down local village traditions everywhere except in Albania, and exposed young women to new experiences that made simple return to old patterns of life unacceptable.

On top of this, millions of Europeans were killed, so that when economic expansion got into high gear in the late 1950s, the local supply of underemployed rural youths, upon which west European cities had always counted to fill their meaner jobs, was inadequate. Communist countries prohibited emigration, since the governments wished to use their rural population as a labor reservoir for planned industrial expansion on the Soviet model. Yugoslavia, in this as much else, became exceptional in permitting its citizens to emigrate, as was also true of the poorer Mediterranean lands – southern Italy, Greece, Spain, and Portugal. These countries were able to supply west European cities (also Australia, Canada, and the United States) with low-skilled labor for a while. Such immigrants were, however, far more alien in their new environment than villagers from close by had been in earlier ages; and when recruitment expanded still further afield to attract Turks and Algerians, Indonesians, Pakistanis, West Africans, and others to the cities of western Europe, no one supposed that assimilation to the host society would or could occur, at least not in the foreseeable future.

In Germany and other central European countries, careful official regulation of immigration from Mediterranean and Moslem lands was intended to prevent exploitation and facilitate the matching of supply and demand for labor by allowing a stipulated number of alien workers to come temporarily. No doubt it did have that effect, defining minimum wage rates and conditions of labor. It also had the effect of separating the immigrants from the host society by giving them a distinct legal status as sojourners in an alien land, who were expected to maintain their native identity, pending return to their country of origin. Many conformed to official expectation by going home after some months or years abroad; but many others preferred to remain, even in periods of economic difficulty, when unemployment reared its ugly head. Moreover, humble jobs that had been filled by alien immigrants often seemed no longer fit for native-born citizens.

Such attitudes, if allowed to persist, would produce permanent differentiation between immigrants and native-born inhabitants. Official policy has not really come to grips with this prospect. It is, of course, impossible to say for sure what the future will bring, but as long as diffential birthrates remain as great as they are between west European and nearby Moslem populations, the old-fashioned ethnically unitary nation is unlikely to be restored.

Even in Britain and France, where an indelible separate legal status was not pinned upon immigrants, the tacit liberal expectation of an eventual assimilation of newcomers to the national norm wilted rapidly in the postwar decades, especially for those groups who were readily distinguishable from the environing population, in physical appearance. The experience of the United States was important here, for in the 1950s Americans emphatically abandoned the ideal of assimilation in favor of a rather more strenuous ideal of somehow combining enduring ethnic multiplicity with legal and social equality for all. Public efforts to equalize income and status between Blacks and whites met with very limited success though some forms of racial discrimination were removed or diminished. In the 1950s and 1960s, the British and French were less exercised over their new minorities than were the Americans, partly because numbers were smaller and immigrants more timorous in asserting any sort of collective self-consciousness. More recently, Black and other visible minorities have become more assertive, at least in Britain; but what direction governmental policy will take remains unclear.

The long-term fate of American, French, and British experiments in polyethnic living remain just as problematic as is the future of the two-tiered society generated by the legal status of *Gastarbeiter* in Germany and Switzerland. Equality and freedom to be different are difficult to reconcile, especially when traditional cultural characteristics and patterns of education fit ethnic groups for some jobs and disqualify them for others. Moreover, even if the competing ideals of liberty and equality should achieve satisfactory resolution among the prevailing mix of ethnic groups, differential rates of population growth, and panic flight from political violence, can be counted on to generate new waves of migrants seeking entry to countries that are richer and freer than their homelands; and such migrants, if admitted, will bring new diversity and establish a still more complex ethnic hierarchy in western Europe and North America than anything that now exists.

Illegal immigrants who abound in the United States, coming mostly from Mexico and from some of the Caribbean islands, already demonstrate the dilemma confronting a country officially committed to equality and liberty. Official efforts to prohibit or regulate migration can do much to control the magnitude and direction of these demographic tides, but cannot turn them on and off at will. Checking illegal migration into the United States, for example, would require an expansion of police power which many Americans are reluctant to accept; yet connivance in illegal immigration, such as now occurs, invites the sort of two-tiered society the Germans have inadvertently created with their *Gastarbeiter*, with the difference that American laws do not protect illegal immigrants from mistreatment as systematically as German regulations do.

These political and sociological dilemmas reflect improvements in communications and transport that continually nibble away at once formidable geographical obstacles to human interaction at a distance. In the nineteenth century and before, moving to a foreign country meant cutting close ties with the homeland for years if not forever. Modern conditions make it possible even for very humble immigrant workers to keep in touch with their place of origin by returning for vacations and telephoning relatives with news and gossip of the kind that used only to be exchanged locally. Such links mean that immigrants find it far easier to maintain their cultural identity in a strange land. Psychologically they remain at home even when away from home; or more exactly, they are able to inhabit two different worlds simultaneously, dealing part of the time with aliens and part of the time with familiars, even if some of their familiars happen to live in another country, many miles away.

Human communities, in other words, are becoming at least partially detachable from geography. This is an old phenomenon: as old as civilization perhaps, inasmuch as written texts allowed sacred truths to transcend both time and distance. But in earlier ages, only small elites participated actively in such communication, and ties among elites were slender since contacts at a distance had to overcome difficult obstacles. Such obstacles have now been reduced to the point that in the richer countries of the earth, at any rate, nearly everyone can keep in touch with kinfolk and friends at will, whether that means communicating across oceans and continents or simply down the road.

Large organizations, too, communicate at will around the globe. Multinational corporations can reallocate resources as seems best to their managers, seeking cheap labor or advantageous legal regulations wherever they are to be found. Such activity characteristically creates a rather different mingling of peoples, in which immigrants occupy the high-skill positions as managers and experts while locally recruited people fill the low-skilled jobs.

The military services of the two great powers, likewise, move across national borders with an ease and on a scale unknown before airplanes and electronic communications achieved their present capacities. Garrisons stationed permanently, or at least for an indefinite future, on foreign soil constitute another significant form of polyethnicity. Sometimes, military personnel are kept severely apart, as happens with Soviet forces stationed in eastern Europe. Sometimes encapsulation in a separate military society is far weaker, as for most American garrisons. But no matter what the legal and social barriers may be, foreign soldiers and host communities inevitably interact with each other in ways no one can fully control or foresee.

Within Europe itself, modern military management

has created the curious circumstance whereby institutions once firmly identified with the innermost arcanum of the nation have themselves become international. In their higher management both NATO and the Warsaw Pact no longer reflect the will of any single nation, not even the dominant partner. Decisions about weaponry and tactics are no longer national but international. Higher headquarters mingle officers and men from different countries. Training exercises, when they assume a large scale, become international as well. Even the French withdrawal from NATO in 1964, aimed at maintaining full sovereignty over their armed forces, was only partially effective, since strategic consultation was never broken off, and a complex tangle of agreements, coordinating French with other European armed forces, was soon restored.

The internationalization of military administration among the most powerful states of the earth and the capacity of large multinational corporations to transcend national borders alike attest to the expansion of the geographical scale of management beyond older limits which once made European nation-states an efficient unit of sovereignty. It is ironic to realize that the peoples of other parts of the earth, especially those subjected to European colonial government before the wars, have been putting considerable energy and hope into the enormous task of constituting national states for themselves, exactly at a time when that scale of political organization was proving inadequate in the place of its birth, that is, in western Europe. Sovereignty which remains fragile and partly fictitious is a poor thing indeed; yet most of the new states of Africa, Asia, and Oceania, together with the older states of Latin America, despite their legal pretensions to sovereign status, continue to depend on foreign loans, foreign weapons, and often also on foreign skills for those things the ruling elites most value, i.e., the signs and symbols of modernity and of power which validate the legitimacy of their governance and social leadership.

The human and material costs of creating a single people within old colonial boundaries are often very great, as massacres in Cambodia and the wholesale expulsion of Indians from east Africa may remind us. And, ironically, the most strenuous efforts at homogenizing local populations through education, road-building, and exposure to governmentally managed radio and TV broadcasts are often accompanied by policies that accord legal privileges to specially skilled foreigners and to foreign corporations, thereby restoring polyethnicity in a particularly painful form to a society attempting to suppress it.

The alternative of excluding foreigners and refusing loans, whether for weapons or for peaceable use, condemns the government and people concerned to continued weakness and poverty, wherever local skills remain far behind those of the world's leaders. Real independence is feasible, perhaps, in countries like Brazil, India, and China, where skills are already high and the national domain vast. It is even possible in Iran, by dint of the fact that the shahs deliberately imported foreign skills on a massive scale, beginning in the 1920s.

Yet autarky remains very costly, even for well-endowed nations, as China's example of revolutionary withdrawal followed by a deliberate return to international exchanges attests. The Soviet Union and its east European allies, also, owe some of the inefficiency of their economic systems to the autarky upon which their governments insist because it makes planning and policing so much easier, whatever the cost in productivity.

Political resistance to intermingling of peoples and skills across state boundaries is therefore far from negligible, and may well increase in time to come as the difficulties of living in polyethnic societies become more widely apparent. The recent riots in Great Britain are a sample of what must be expected when different ethnic groups bring sharp cultural differences into immediate juxtaposition by migrating into city slums. Nothing assures that the assortment of migrants and their skills will fit smoothly into the host society. Indeed, market rhythms of boom and bust assure that periods of labor shortage will alternate with periods of labor surplus; and the groups most at risk in periods of economic downturn are usually the most recently arrived. Yet going back home is not always a feasible alternative for immigrants in times of hardship; and even the most carefully calculated public policies cannot foresee the future well enough to assure a smooth adjustment of supply and demand for labor by shuttling workers back and forth between host country and their native villages. People resist being herded about like sheep; and bureaucratic wisdom – not to say justice – is in too short supply to allow us to rely confidently on what would amount to a new, collectivized system of intermittent indentured labor. Yet private decisions, made on the basis of very imperfect information, confront the same uncertain future and have no chance of foreseeing the full consequences of a decision to emigrate or to stay home instead.

It would be silly to expect certainty or predictability in myriad human encounters provoked by modern transport and communications, acting in concert with the demographic dynamic of our time, and the tides of thought and feeling that run so tumultuously among us. It would be even more absurd to expect that ethnic unity within separate, sovereign national states would remain or, rather, become normal in such an interacting world. Yet, unexamined, our heritage inclines us to make that assumption. Mental inertia and the capacity we all have of seeing only what we wish to see and glossing over anything that contradicts our preferences may well continue to support pretense of ethnic unity within sovereign national states for some time to come. But the reality is otherwise and becoming more so with each decade. Polyethnic hierarchy is on the rise, everywhere.

So far, efforts to sustain equality in face of actual differences in skill and custom have met with very limited success. For those of us who value civic freedom and equality such a record, and the testimony of the past, are or ought to be troubling. Other civilized societies have almost always accepted and enforced inequality among the diverse ethnic groups of which they were composed. In the Roman empire, Stoic ideas of Cosmopolis, whose citizenry was universal simply by virtue of its shared humanity, did indeed enjoy currency among an educated minority, and may even have played some part in the legal extension of Roman citizenship to all free men of the empire in 212 AD. But the tax liabilities that went along with citizenship were what the imperial authorities were really thinking about, almost for sure.

Religious universalism, whether Buddhist, Christian, or Moslem, also insists on the equality of all true believers; but that idea does not interfere with actual differentiation along sectarian and ethnic lines within as well as between adherents of these faiths. In a sense, Confucian reliance on assigning high social status on the strength of a specialized education, validated by passing standardized written examinations, was more egalitarian than any other traditional social system, and easily bridged ethnic differences by converting anyone who mastered the classics into a Chinese. Yet the gap between rulers and ruled in Confucian China was enormous. Instead of citizenship, everyone except the emperor himself was a subject with a duly appointed rank which it was the emperor's duty to supervise and sustain by example and, when necessary, by force.

The participatory equality of the classical city-states, from which our ideas of political freedom descend, was transitory, however glorious. And citizenship in those ancient city-states was a privilege, limited to free men, who were also the sons of citizens. Immigrant foreigners, when they existed, were excluded; so were women and slaves. Modern national states of the liberal tradition accepted foreigners as at least potential citizens; and women, too, achieved political rights, though only in the twentieth century. Whether these principles will survive the impact of an interacting world in which vast differences of skills, culture, wealth, and physical appearance exist is one of the capital questions for the next century.

Very likely things will muddle along for decades to come. Preaching apocalyptic disaster is easy, but has almost always turned out to be wrong. But social strains and frictions are almost sure to increase within nations playing host to different ethnic groups; and sporadic resort to riot and even to wholesale murder is likely. It is a high price to pay for open frontiers; yet the costs of artificial isolation and of maintaining ethnic purity by the exercise of force are even greater. Civilized peoples have confronted this awkward choice from the beginning of urban existence. We and our successors will continue to wrestle with the difficulty of living with others who are different from ourselves in greater or lesser ways, and at greater or lesser distances. Accommodation to others, who are also alien, is one dimension of the human condition, and always has been.

The peculiar balance between homogeneity and diversity that a few west European nations were able to strike in the late eighteenth century and maintained until the twentieth was a phase – a passing phase – remarkable and admirable in many respects, but oppressive and repugnant from the viewpoint of those over whom they exercised imperial authority. The ethnically unitary European nation-state never existed except as an ideal. Since the world wars of this century, it has plainly become obsolete in the place of its birth. It can scarcely be taken as a viable model any longer. Polyethnicity in some form or other is preferable, despite all its drawbacks and difficulties.

Canadian and American experience gives North America something of a head start in the awkward matter of getting used to living side by side with people of differing ethnic heritage. Europeans are only beginning to get used to looking across the Atlantic; but in matters of public policy towards ethnic minorities they may have reason to do so in time to come. At the very least, Canadians and Americans can take some comfort in realizing that our domestic ethnic frictions are a cost of participating in the modern world from which no people or government, not even the Japanese, can long remain immune.

If I am right, such frictions are not, as nationalists like Donald Creighton assumed, due to a regrettable lag in nation-building. In appearing before you in his name, I am therefore debating with him, challenging his views, treading roughly on some of his most cherished ideals. I recognize the impiety of my behavior and only hope that, were he alive, the man in whose honor these lectures are held would relish the irony and accept the compliment implied in arguing against him, as I have done.